*cui dono lepidum novum libellum*
*arida modo pumice expolitum*

To whom should I present this little book
just now polished with a pumice stone?

# Bad Kid
# CATULLUS

sidekickBOOKS

First published in 2017 by

SIDEKICK BOOKS
42 Silvester Road
London SE22 9PB

Printed by
The Russell Press

Typeset in Vollkorn and Gill Sans

~

ISBN: 978-1-909560-25-3

Cover art and design by Jon Stone

dEVS·QVEM·ʃ

# HOW TO USE THIS BOOK

Read it. Write in it. Take it with you.

Make it your own.

The scabrous, self-contradictory poems of Gaius Valerius Catullus have been revisited many times before, and it's always been a messy affair. But never more messy than this – we've thrown the concept of the faithful translation to the wind, and let versions of these works grow weird and wild and shaggy and thorny. None of us are Latin scholars, so you have no reason to trust us.

What's more, we've left plenty of room for you to join in the debauchery. Follow or ignore the suggested exercises as you wish, edit or delete the existing pieces, write in the borders or glue in additional pages with honey – but whatever you do, stuff this book to the brim, until it's so full of vice and voluptuousness that you feel compelled to hide it from visiting relatives. There's surely no better way to summon and entertain the spirit of Catullus.

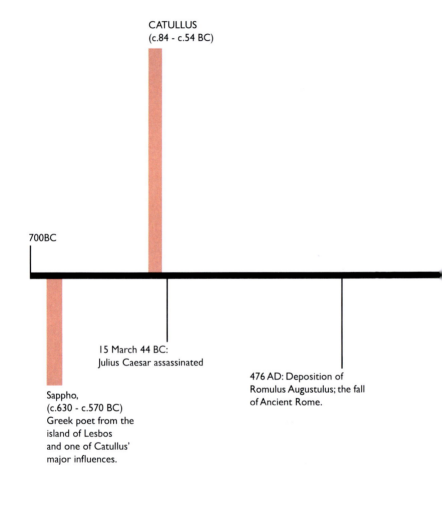

CATULLUS
(c.84 - c.54 BC)

700BC

15 March 44 BC:
Julius Caesar assassinated

476 AD: Deposition of
Romulus Augustulus; the fall
of Ancient Rome.

Sappho,
(c.630 - c.570 BC)
Greek poet from the
island of Lesbos
and one of Catullus'
major influences.

HOMO VRBANVS DVAS
TANTXM RES OPTAT
AMOREM ET VERSVS

966: Bishop Ratherius of
Verona discovers a manuscript
of Catullus' poems and
"reproache[s] himself for
spending day and night" with it.

1472: First print edition of
Catulllus' poems produced
in Venice.

2017

More translations and
scholarly articles on Catullus
produced than kisses he
planted on women and men
combined.

Geoffrey Chaucer (c. 1343 - 1400)
*from* The Miller's Tale:
*Derk was the nyght as pich, or as a cole,*
*And at the wyndow out she putte hir hole,*
*And Absolon, hym fil no bet ne wers,*
*But with his mouth he kiste hir naked ers*

1489: Poliziano is the first
scholar to conjecture that
Catulllus' sparrow is a
metaphor for his penis.

# BRIEF RECONSTRUCTED BIOGRAPHY:

**Approx. 84BC** Gaius Valerius Catullus born to a wealthy family in Verona. Native of Cisalpine Gaul (Gaul This Side of the Alps).

**Approx. 65BC** Buys a fixer-upper flat in Sirmio, the modern Sirmione, on Lake Garda. Does very little fixing up, preferring instead to write poetry, or *carmina*.

**Approx. 64BC** Tiring of country life, buys a villa near the Roman suburb of Tibur, which is 'up and coming' with good, straight roads. Frequents an artisanal fig eatery and complains about gaulification.

**57BC** Travels to Bithynia in Asia Minor in the retinue of Gaius Memmius, the Roman governor of the province. Visits his brother's grave. Best friend Cinna goes along too and convinces Catullus to buy a yacht while drunk.

**57BC** Returns to Sirmio with Cinna in new yacht. Remortgages Roman villa to pay for yacht.

**57BC** Meets the lover he nicknames Lesbia, and begins a tumultuous love affair spanning 25 poems and 513 boxes of consolatory honey cakes.

**57BC** Meets and begins affair with Juventus, a handsome youth.

**56BC** Writes XI, in which he calls Caesar "shameless, greedy, a gambler" for patronising the wealthy engineer Mamurra.

**56BC** Apologises after a sharp word from his father, a very good friend of Caesar.

**56BC** Writes LVII ("You Two!"), which portrays Caesar and Mamurra as sodomite and catamite. Calls them "beautifully matched" and "perverse little buggers".

**56BC** Apologises after a strongly worded letter from Caesar's Pleb Relations scribes.

**56BC** Writes in XCIII:
"I couldn't care less about impressing you, Caesar,
or knowing whether you dress left or right."

**56BC** Apologises. Is invited to dinner with Caesar the same day. Accepts but makes it clear to friends he's going for research purposes. Several other poets complain about not being invited.

**Approx.54BC** Catullus dies, aged around 30. 116 of his carmina survive today.

"From the first line it should be clear that Catullus does not care a fig what his readers think of his piety and chastity from reading his verses …"

Thomas Nelson Winter, *Catullus Purified: A Brief History of Carmen 16*

"His choice of what to say and what to leave out gives the reader a different impression than if the conversation was related from, say, Lesbia's point of view."

Rebecca Read, *Catullus the Conversationalist: A Study of the Relationship between Narrator and Reader*

## reviews from *Goodreads.com*:

"i relate to catullus bc i too am petty, bitter, overdramatic & bisexual."

Charlotte

"If nothing else, Catullus knew how to want things. And where is all of it now?"

Douglas

"It is both rude and beautiful."

James

"I found it very difficult not to like this fellow, this apolitical Roman playboy who survives to us as much from luck as from skill as a poet."

Abraham

CATVLLVS POEMA DECENS VIX HABET

↗

GEORGIVS GORDONVS HOC SCRIPSIT

# I. THE POEMS
## various versions,
## mutations
## and departures

LESBIA POST·HOC·VSVS.

## Layout

Poem number

# IIb

Original
Latin

TAM gratum est mihi quam ferunt puellae
pernici aureolum fuisse malum,
quod zonam soluit diu ligatam.

Versions
and translations

*1904 version*
*Francis Warre Cornish*

This is as grateful to me as to the swift maiden was (they say) the golden apple, which loosed her girdle too long tied.

**"** Catullus has chosen the myth of Atalanta because it fits both his situation and Lesbia's and thus allows him to say more than he expresses. **"**

Lee T. Pearcy, *Catullus 2B: Or Not 2B?*

Fragment of piercing scholarly insight

MEI · HAS TAM · TENDAT · IN · TE

# II

PASSER, deliciae meae puellae,

quicum ludere, quem in sinu tenere,

cui primum digitum dare appetenti

et acris solet incitare morsus,

cum desiderio meo nitenti

carum nescio quid lubet iocari

et solaciolum sui doloris,

credo ut tum gravis acquiescat ardor:

tecum ludere sicut ipsa possem

et tristis animi levare curas!

*1904 version*
*Francis Warre Cornish*

Sparrow, my lady's pet, with whom she often plays and holds you in her bosom, or gives you her finger-tip to peck and teases you to bite sharply, whenever she, the bright-shining lady of my love, has a fancy for some dear dainty toying, that (as I think) when the sharper pangs of love abate, she may find some small solace of her pain—ah, might I but play with you as she herself does, and lighten the gloomy cares of my heart!

*In six words:*

I could use a temporary distraction.

## Catullus 2
### Jei Degenhardt

O Cato,
and other name-
dropping, Lesbia,
called Clytemnestra knockoff
  can you tell I'm drunk—
sparrow woman with her bird it pecked her
which she liked it pecked me which she liked more
*in sinu tenere*, which means she holds it round against her,
fingercage,
    tender,
 'Can you reach that apple?' she said, pointing.
  'Sparrow can.' (*Passer* means sparrow, pet name, sometimes ostrich,
like the feather I can't balance) Or with more mercy,
  'You've got sand on your eyelashes.'
*angiportis* [alleyway] she's been
down many, a bird told me – Lesbia says,
  'Sure, but birds don't speak
                        to you.'
Hate-love
I call myself *tristis* (gloomy) and you
point out it's another bird
 'Grey crow, pretty little thing.
    You can even teach them to talk.'

**"** That sparrow of Catullus in my opinion allegorically
conceals a certain more obscene meaning (...) What
this is, for the modesty of my pen, I leave to each
reader to conjecture from the native salaciousness
of the sparrow. **"**

Angelo Poliziano

Sparrow! my pet, delicious joy,

Wherewith in bosom wast toy

She loves, and gives the finger-tip

For sharp-nib'd greeting neck to nip,

Were she who may desire withstood

To seek some pet of merry mood,

As LOVE! a comfort for her grief

Methinks her burning love's relief

Could I, as plays she, play with thee

That mind might turn from misery free!

me twere grateful (as they say)

Gold sealing was to fleet-foot play,

Whose long-bound zone it loosed for

homo lupic homo homin.

## Address to a Bird

Write a poem or letter to a bird you regularly encounter – in your garden, on your windowsill, on your way to work or otherwise. Read it aloud when your paths next cross. Bonus points for bewildered bystanders. Bonus points if the bird stands for someone or something other than itself.

*(left) Staves version*
*Vahni Capildeo*

# III

Lvgete, o Veneres Cupidinesque,
et quantum est hominum venustiorum:
passer mortuus est meae puellae,
passer, deliciae meae puellae,
quem plus illa oculis suis amabat.
nam mellitus erat suamque norat
ipsam tam bene quam puella matrem,
nec sese a gremio illius movebat,
sed circumsiliens modo huc modo illuc
ad solam dominam usque pipiabat.
qui nunc it per iter tenebricosum
illuc, unde negant redire quemquam.
at vobis male sit, malae tenebrae
Orci, quae omnia bella devoratis:
tam bellum mihi passerem abstulistis
o factum male! o miselle passer!
tua nunc opera meae puellae
flendo turgiduli rubent ocelli.


*In six words:*

Send help: sparrow dead, girl inconsolable.

## A LAMENTATION ON THE SPARROW'S DEATH

MOURN all ye Loves! ye Graces mourn!
My Lesbia's fav'rite sparrow's gone!
Ye men for wit, for taste, preferr'd,
Lament my girl's departed bird!
That sparrow, than her eyes more dear,
Which oft has charm'd her list'ning ear;
Which knew her, as the infant knows
The breast, from whence its being flows;
Which, hopping in amusive sport,
At her lov'd side would pay its court;
And, seated on her bosom's throne,
Would pipe to her, and her alone:
Poor bird! who now that darksome bourn
Hast pass'd, whence none can e'er return:
Perish ye shades of Stygian gloom,
Which all that's elegant consume!
'Twas you, detested be the day!
Who snatch'd our charming bird away;
O hapless bird! o fatal deed!
That makes my Lesbia's bosom bleed;
And, her eyes swoll'n with many a tear,
Bids the red streak of grief appear.

**" We might, however, reasonably wonder whether Catullus curses [the spirits of the underworld] for ruining his *puella*'s looks by making her cry (...) rather than for the death of the sparrow. "**

J. Ingleheart, *Catullus 2 and 3: A Pair of Sapphic Epigrams?*

Weep every Venus, and
And men who of short duration, is still prevail.
Dead is the Sparrow of my girl, the joy,
Sparrow, my sweeting's most delicious to
Whom loved she do      her v    yes;
For he    s honeyed-pe
Knew     r a      she
Ne'er    he    his h
But r    d her hopping here
Piped he to none but hi

*Mean peak frequency was 55 kHz.*

*two strong harmonics.*

*Echolocation:*

*Echolocation:*

*the bat*

*Echolocation:*

*of branch diameter as a limiting factor in attacks*
*of this species flying*

Thither whence Life-return t
But ah! *This bat produces FM echolocation pulses*
In Orcus e
Who bore
(Oh ha
Now
Wi

*an arboreal bird-blood specialist.*
*stomach contents has in fact shown th*

*White-winged*

*Vampire*

*Bat*

*Desmodus young?*

*Sparrow for he taen*
— and Oh deed of bane!
enter work my girl appears
opens its mouth    tears.

MOR    US!!!   AMABAT

*; when disturbed*
mellit
O! erat    O!    O!    O!

PIPIABAT    PIPIABAT

## *Lamentation*

Consider the death of an animal. It may be one that was your companion, or the companion to a friend. It may be one you saw dead on the road once, or one that was killed in front of you. Kindle your sorrow, and compose your lament. Read it to a friend.

*(left) Collage version*
*Vahni Capildeo*

*Catullus og Lesbia, der i hans arme søger trøst for hendes spurvs død. (Catullus and Lesbia, who in his arms seeks solace for the death of her sparrow.)*
*Nicolai Abildgaard (1743-1809)*
*1809, oil on canvas*

## *Caption competition*

Come up with some captions for the painting opposite. Enlist such help as is needed from family and friends.

# V

VIVAMVS mea Lesbia, atque amemus,
rumoresque senum severiorum
omnes unius aestimemus assis!
soles occidere et redire possunt:
nobis cum semel occidit brevis lux,
nox est perpetua una dormienda.
da mi basia mille, deinde centum,
dein mille altera, dein secunda centum,
deinde usque altera mille, deinde centum.
dein, cum milia multa fecerimus,
conturbabimus illa, ne sciamus,
aut ne quis malus inuidere possit,
cum tantum sciat esse basiorum.

*In six words:*

Kisses, Lesbia! Squillions of them, stat!

Let us live, my Lesbia, and love, and value at one farthing all the talk of crabbed old men.

Suns may set and rise again. For us, when the short light has once set, remains to be slept the sleep of one unbroken night.

Give me a thousand kisses, then a hundred, then another thousand, then a second hundred, then yet another thousand, then a hundred. Then, when we have made up many thousands, we will confuse our counting, that we may not know the reckoning, nor any malicious person blight them with evil eye, when he knows that our kisses are so many.

66 It was a brilliant stroke on Catullus' part to combine the ardent passion of the lover with the hardheadedness of the businessman ... 99

Richard E. Grimm, *Catullus 5 Again*

*Shake It Off* – Taylor Swift (2014)
*It Don't Mean a Thing (If It Ain't Got That Swing)*
                             – Duke Ellington (1930)
*Days Go By* – Dirty Vegas (2001)
*When the Sun Goes Down* – Arctic Monkeys (2006)
*It's Gonna Be a Long Night* – Gerry Rafferty (1979)
*Kiss* – Prince (1986)
*Kiss Me* – Sixpence None The Richer (1998)
*Let Me Kiss You* – Morrissey (2008)
*Keep Them Kisses Comin'* – Craig Campbell (2013)
*A Hundred Kisses* – She Wants Revenge (2008)
*A Thousand Kisses Deep* – Leonard Cohen (2001)
*One More Kiss* – Wings (1973)
*How Many Times* – Bob Marley and the Wailers (1968)
*A Heavy Abacus* – The Joy Formidable (2011)
*Smash It Up* – The Damned (1979)

*Clocks magazine version*
*Abi Palmer*

**44** Diary of a
clock repairer

Let us really live, my Lesbia, that is to say, let us love,

for us, take the goats home, shut up the calves

and all the muttering of old clock and watch enthusiasts

let us value at one cent! I am greatly puzzled by the iron dial.

of the 'chest-suns' worn by Yukaghir girls I am not so naive.).

Suns can set and rise;

PERHAPS I can assist

As every cat owner knows

when once this evanescent light sets,

...WE ANSWER

one eternal night must be AMATEURS CORNER

Perhaps this was the reason behind The conversion.

Give me a thousand kisses, then a hundred

CLOCKS CLOCKS / CLOCKS Clocks CLOCKS

then another thousand, then a battery operated clock

then straight on to another thousand, then a hundred

screw-drivers,

Then, when we have added up many thousands,

neither man nor tree is recognisable,

we will go bankrupt, lest we know a hole big enough to

give me particulars

or lest anyone wicked can cast the evil eye,

inasmuch as he knows what the total of our kisses are.

*Lesbia's Reply*
*Vahni Capildeo*

Was a time, Catullus, i'd indulge
your counting fetish.
relay how long
                   a pause
                              i'd need
ascending stairs
              to bed:
squidge. wipe. repeat.
sensation strigilled my declining body.
switched on hyper sensitivities
to linen thread. count.
not to say stone.
till skin inclined to flinch from
sucking-disks. remora-like. which swarm.
from any contact. every surface.
you write when you're cross.
                                   sharp. silk.
you're a cultured man.
                        dressing
made to measure.
                  rubbing
those bronze balls on your abacus.
spittle kissing mercury
on your practice-mirror.
as for me:
         i'm lying
                   open,
                              beautifully open,
to a tease of a beautician's
innumerable tweezings.
laughing with the blonde from Gallia
who lays her head
low on my belly
while she tends my lady-garden.

## *Journal of Osculations*

Put an X on this page every time you kiss someone, until the page is full. Embellish the record with notes on the timing, or the sensation.

# VII

QVAERIS, quot mihi basiationes
tuae, Lesbia, sint satis superque.
quam magnus numerus Libyssae harenae
lasarpiciferis iacet Cyrenis
oraclum Iovis inter aestuosi
et Batti veteris sacrum sepulcrum;
aut quam sidera multa, cum tacet nox,
furtivos hominum vident amores:
tam te basia multa basiare
vesano satis et super Catullo est,
quae nec pernumerare curiosi
possint nec mala fascinare lingua.

**" Yet in this poem sand and stars do not function simply as quantitative symbols. Each is in fact described in a manner that subtly alludes to the mouth ... "**

Stephen Bertman, *Oral Imagery in Catullus 7*

*Carmina Sutra*
*Position 7: The Waterfall*
*Jon Stone*

How
many? As
in, to sate
me, to over
whelm me?
Oh, I don't know,
let's say about
as many     as
there   are itty
grains  of sand tucked between
Jupiter's sweaty oracle    and
old Battus' holy catacomb. *Or,*
say, *as many as the spying, prying*          *pin*
*pri*c*k* s*t*ars *in a soundless*       *night, gazing down on*
*all these,* mm, *steamy*              *sweet hook-ups*
*in the streets* and
h        *ouses. Yeah,*    that
*seems the right amount to*      me,
*mad old Catullus. More*
*kisses        than you*
*can            count.*
*More than you could*
*curse.*

## Lesbia's Reply
### Kate Wakeling

Count on this. It didn't take a wicked tongue.

No curse. No foe. Reckon only yourself

to blame. That fevered need to test, to tot up

what might instead, let loose, have sprung and seeded

in its dizzy, gentle way. On asking how

many would be enough I did not want this

poesied list of stars and sands, a chattered quest,

summing kisses as your stilted   curative

because  without because    the soundless thread

where trust quivers  tenses holds the      I know

you watched  me  while         I         slept      I am

exhausted by your       digits at my throat

## *Things there are a lot of*

Teeth in the heads of all the crocodiles in all of Africa. Gigabytes of data in a human ballsack. Hazardous waste, in tons, dumped into the ocean every year. Keep the list going until the page is full.

# VIII

Miser Catulle, desinas ineptire,
et quod vides perisse perditum ducas.
Fulsere quondam candidi tibi soles,
cum ventitabas quo puella ducebat
amata nobis quantum amabitur nulla.
Ibi illa multa cum iocosa fiebant,
quae tu volebas nec puella nolebat,
fulsere vere candidi tibi soles.
Nunc iam illa non vult: tu quoque impotens noli,
nec quae fugit sectare, nec miser vive,
sed obstinata mente perfer, obdura.
Vale puella, iam Catullus obdurat,
nec te requiret nec rogabit invitam.
At tu dolebis, cum rogaberis nulla.
Scelesta, uae te, quae tibi manet uita?
Quis nunc te adibit? cui videberis bella?
Quem nunc amabis? Cuius esse diceris?
Quem basiabis? Cui labella mordebis?
At tu, Catulle, destinatus obdura.


*In six words:*

Dammit, Catullus, forget the stupid girl.

*19th Century English Slang Version*
*Rowyda Amin*

To Himself ragging Lesbia's being Hunt's dog.
Blubbering Catullus! Cease to play the noddy
And what thou seest backed as kickerapoo regard!
It was nuts for the cull and mort
When all-a-gog whither led the well-rigged frigate,

My chuck, as shall no dodsey be loved.
There all so peppery doings then were done
After thy liking, nor the rum doxy was loath.
Then thou simpered like a furmity kettle.
Now it's against her pluck: thou too (cagged!) will

Come home by weeping cross.
Wear the willow not budging from hence.
Blowen, I'm off! Catullus eats cold pudding,
Won't shove a trunk, neither blast your top lights;
Yet shalt thou sing the black psalm.

Jade! Blue devils to thee! What life remains?
What rum duke shall dock thee? Who'll think thee dimber?
Whom now shalt join giblets? Whose lawful blanket be called?
To whom shalt smacks give? Whose gan nip?
But thou (Catullus!) shut your bone box and die game.

*from* The Carmina of Gaius Valerius Catullus *(trans. Richard Burton and Leonard Smithers), and Captain Grose's 1811* Dictionary of the Vulgar Tongue.

## Secutor v Retiarius (Gladiator Version)
### Kirsten Irving

Catullus, focus! For the crowd if not yourself.
You know a moment's sighing or sniffing,
will see you speared and drained on the sand.
A week back, I was Mars in the flesh
before this Fury with her whirling net
snagged my sword, held me by the hilt.
laid me out flat, and saw that I liked it.
The sun growled down and heated my helmet.
Now she's taken her snare and swagger
and I cannot refuse to fight any but her.
Cannot cry my hat rusty. Can only grimace.
So long, my Invidia. Stoneheart Catullus
is a blinkered horse who sees only the road.
No doubt you'll miss the howl of his blade.
No doubt you'll practise your semi-clad jig
alone on a beach, with no one to praise you.
There will be no crowds. No title to snatch.
No iron-head partner, no muscle to slit.
I will hold up my shield against your echo.

" He must give up his beloved as lost to him. He
cannot. But he must. (…) His awareness of his
ridiculous situation is clarified by the metric,
the invective cadence of which is directed as
much to his wounded, limping self as to his
inconstant beloved … "

Roy Arthur Swanson, *The Humor of Catullus 8*

## *Auto-address*

Write an extremely stern letter to yourself, attempting to dissuade you from a bad habit or destructive preoccupation. Photocopy the page and pin the copy to your fridge. Points for every house guest who is subsequently shocked, shaken or horribly intrigued.

# XI

FVRI et Aureli comites Catulli,
sive in extremos penetrabit Indos,
litus ut longe resonante Eoa
tunditur unda,
sive in Hyrcanos Arabesue molles,
seu Sagas sagittiferosue Parthos,
sive quae septemgeminus colorat
aequora Nilus,
sive trans altas gradietur Alpes,
Caesaris visens monimenta magni,
Gallicum Rhenum horribile aequor ulti-
mosque Britannos,
omnia haec, quaecumque feret voluntas
caelitum, temptare simul parati,
pauca nuntiate meae puellae
non bona dicta.
cum suis vivat valeatque moechis,
quos simul complexa tenet trecentos,
nullum amans vere, sed identidem omnium
ilia rumpens;
nec meum respectet, ut ante, amorem,
qui illius culpa cecidit uelut prati
ultimi flos, praetereunte postquam
tactus aratro est.

*In six words:*

Tell my ultra-slutty girlfriend it's over.

*1904 version*
*Francis Warre Cornish*

Furius and Aurelius, who will be Catullus' fellow travellers, whether he makes his way as far as to the distant Indies, where the shore is beaten by the farresounding eastern wave, or to the Hyrcanians and soft Arabs, or Sacae and archer Parthians, or the plains which sevenfold Nile discolours, or whether he will tramp across the high Alps, to visit the memorials of great Caesar, the Gaulish Rhine, the formidable and remotest Britons, – O my friends, ready as you are to encounter all these risks with me, whatever the will of the gods above shall bring, take a little message, not a kind message, to my mistress. Bid her live and be happy with her paramours, three hundred of whom she holds at once in her embrace, not loving one of them really, but again and again breaking the strength of all. And let her not look to find my love, as before; my love, which by her fault has dropped, like a flower on the meadow's edge, when it has been touched by the plough passing by.

“ The irony of a man who could once talk of facing the *ultimos Britannos* being transformed into a fallen flower of the *prati ultimi* is both poignant and poetically masterful. ”

Phyllis Young Forsyth, *The Thematic Unity of Catullus 11*

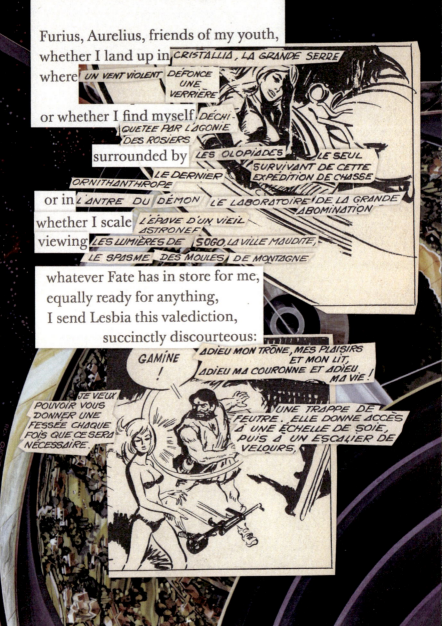

**11**

Furius, Aurelius, friends of my youth,
whether I land up in CRISTALLIA, LA GRANDE SERRE
where UN VENT VIOLENT DÉFONCE UNE VERRIÈRE

or whether I find myself DÉCHI-
QUETÉE PAR L'AGONIE
DES ROSIERS

surrounded by LES OLOPIADES LE SEUL
SURVIVANT DE CETTE
LE DERNIER EXPÉDITION DE CHASSE
ORNITHANTHROPE

or in L'ANTRE DU DÉMON LE LABORATOIRE DE LA GRANDE
ABOMINATION

whether I scale L'ÉPAVE D'UN VIEIL
ASTRONEF
viewing LES LUMIÈRES DE SOGO, LA VILLE MAUDITE,
LE SPASME DES MOULES DE MONTAGNE

whatever Fate has in store for me,
equally ready for anything,
I send Lesbia this valediction,
        succinctly discourteous:

GAMINE
!

ADIEU MON TRÔNE, MES PLAISIRS
ET MON LIT,
ADIEU MA COURONNE ET ADIEU
MA VIE !

JE VEUX
POUVOIR VOUS
DONNER UNE
FESSÉE CHAQUE
FOIS QUE CE SERA
NÉCESSAIRE.

UNE TRAPPE DE
FEUTRE. ELLE DONNE ACCÈS
À UNE ÉCHELLE DE SOIE,
PUIS À UN ESCALIER DE
VELOURS.

*(left) Barbarellus version*
*Jon Stone*

*(below) Mercalli-Richter version*
*Abigail Parry*

## Mercalli Scale

| | | |
|---|---|---|
| I | **Instrumental** | I send Lesbia this valediction, |
| II | **Feeble** | – detected only by seismographs |
| III | **Slight** | live with your three hundred lovers (few people notice) |
| IV | **Moderate** | open your legs to them all – hardly felt |
| V | **Rather strong** | lovelessly dragging the guts out of each of them |
| VI | **Strong** | – sleepers awakened, bells toll |
| VII | **Very strong** | blind to the love that I had for you – trees sway, |
| VIII | **Destructive** | objects fall that you, tart, – general alarm, walls crack |
| IX | **Ruinous** | wantonly crushed – houses fall, ground cracks |
| X | **Disastrous** | as the passing plough-blade slashes the flower |
| XI | **Very disastrous** | – ground opens, landslides |
| XII | **Catastrophic** | at the field's edge. – total destruction |

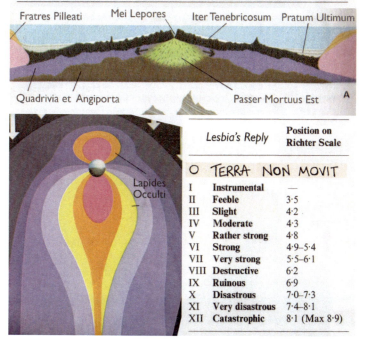

Fratres Pilleati  Mei Lepores  Iter Tenebricosum  Pratum Ultimum

Quadrivia et Angiporta  Passer Mortuus Est  A

Lapides Occulti

| | *Lesbia's Reply* | **Position on Richter Scale** |
|---|---|---|
| O | TERRA NON MOVIT | |
| I | **Instrumental** | — |
| II | **Feeble** | 3·5 |
| III | **Slight** | 4·2 |
| IV | **Moderate** | 4·3 |
| V | **Rather strong** | 4·8 |
| VI | **Strong** | 4·9–5·4 |
| VII | **Very strong** | 5·5–6·1 |
| VIII | **Destructive** | 6·2 |
| IX | **Ruinous** | 6·9 |
| X | **Disastrous** | 7·0–7·3 |
| XI | **Very disastrous** | 7·4–8·1 |
| XII | **Catastrophic** | 8·1 (Max 8·9) |

## Variations on Sexual Invective 1

*nullum amans vere, sed identidem omnium*
*ilia rumpens;*

"wear each lover's strength away, / In brutal lust, in joyless play" (John Nott, 1795); "None truly loving and withal of all / Bursting the vitals" (Sir Richard Francis Burton, 1894); "loving not one in truth, but bursting again and again the flanks of all" (Leonard C. Smithers, 1894); "not loving one of them really, but again and again breaking the strength of all" (Francis Warre Cornish, 1904); "Loving none truly, but leaving them every one / Wrung out & dropping" (W.S. Merwin, 1952); "lovelessly dragging the guts out of each of them" (Peter Whigham, 1966); "Loving none truly but again and again / Rupturing all's groins" (Guy Lee, 1990); "truly loving none of them, but repeatedly breaking the groins of / all of them" (Bryn Stromberg, 1997); "loving none, having all, over and over / just breaking their balls" (Josephine Balmer, 2004); "loving none truly, yet cracking each one's loins / over and over" (Peter Green, 2005); "Loving none truly but repeatedly breaking / All their balls" (Daisy Dunn, 2016); "Truly loving none, but again and again of all the / groins" (Google Translate, 2017)

(Add your own)

## Reconstruction

What little we know about Catullus is gleaned largely from the poems themselves. Draw, or collage, or scrapbook three portraits of him based on your impression thus far.

As supermodel:

As supervillain:

As jongleur:

# XV

COMMENDO tibi me ac meos amores,
Aureli. Veniam peto pudentem,
ut, si quicquam animo tuo cupisti,
quod castum expeteres et integellum,
conserves puerum mihi pudice,
non dico a populo -- nihil veremur
istos, qui in platea modo huc modo illuc
in re praetereunt sua occupati --
verum a te metuo tuoque pene
infesto pueris bonis malisque.
Quem tu qua lubet, ut lubet moveto
quantum vis, ubi erit foris paratum:
hunc unum excipio, ut puto, pudenter.
Quod si te mala mens furorque vecors.
In tantam impulerit, sceleste, culpam,
ut nostrum insidiis caput lacessas.
A tum te miserum malique fati!
Quem attractis pedibus patente porta
percurrent raphanique mugilesque.

*In six words:*

Safeguard my boytoy, A. No shennanigans!

*1894 version*
*Richard Francis Burton*

TO AURELIUS—HANDS OFF THE BOY!

To thee I trust my loves and me,
(Aurelius!) craving modesty.
That (if in mind didst ever long
To win aught chaste unknowing wrong)

Then guard my boy in purest way.
From folk I say not: naught affray
The crowds wont here and there to run
Through street-squares, busied every one;
But thee I dread nor less thy penis

Fair or foul, younglings' foe I ween is!
Wag it as wish thou, at its will,
When out of doors its hope fulfil;
Him bar I, modestly, methinks.
But should ill-mind or lust's high jinks

Thee (Sinner!), drive to sin so dread,
That durst ensnare our dearling's head,
Ah! woe's thee (wretch!) and evil fate,
Mullet and radish shall pierce and grate,
When feet-bound, haled through yawning gate.

(Skip ahead 10 pages to find out if Aurelius obeyed)

15. A Warning: To Aurelius
& if you've ever scumble[aureli
Us]'d yr fuck-tough blubber on the
HIGH HIGHER High(!)eR setting & scabbed
awake to own lone juices en-dank
pouted yr rouge-est of curtains
softer than [monstrous] [aureli
Us]'d if'n you held back ever or read
another's bedsock'd dream of plato
then: SAVE IT. SAVE IT. for some
toy o'er than my 'reverse harvest'
legs cracked apart bright caulked
shake him raw to the rims (though)
put more holes in him I'll slice you
so thin & ~~punch right~~ through

## *Warning Notice*

Consider a rival (past or present) for another person's affection or friendship. Use this page to draft an incendiary letter to your rival, then make a legible copy. Post the copy in a public place.

# XVI

Pedicabo ego vos et irrumabo,
Aureli pathice et cinaede Furi,
qui me ex versiculis meis putastis,
quod sunt molliculi, parum pudicum.
Nam castum esse decet pium poetam
ipsum, versiculos nihil necesse est;
qui tum denique habent salem ac leporem,
si sunt molliculi ac parum pudici,
et quod pruriat incitare possunt,
non dico pueris, sed his pilosis
qui duros nequeunt movere lumbos.
Vos, quod milia multa basiorum
legistis, male me marem putatis?
Pedicabo ego vos et irrumabo.

*In six words:*

Fuck you, Aurelius. Fuck you, Furius.

## Furius and Aurelius: Vexatiously
### Harry Giles

Bag an anal whack and a craw slam,
wang-fans that slap Cat's stanzas
as raw bawd, damn Cat's rap bad as Cat's
a tart. A class act can scrawl art, and
a scandal craftsman can and all;
as a fact, ballads can tang and zap
apart as tart's bacchanals,
and can scratch, can act as match
at hard lads and slack-schwantz granddads.
And stalwart wankshafts scan Cat's "CCC smacks"
and yap that Cat's as a half-mast charlatan?
Cat slams that man's craw, whacks that man's ass.


## 1894/1904 mixed version
### Richard Francis Burton vs. Francis Warre Cornish

I'll —— you twain and ——
Pathic Aurelius! Furius, libertines!
Who have supposed me immodest,
on account of my verses,
because these are rather voluptuous.
For the holy poet ought to be chaste himself,
his verses need not be.
Nay, gain they finally more salt of wit
When over softy and of scanty shame,
Apt for exciting somewhat prurient,
In boys, I say not, but in bearded men
Who fail of movements in their hardened loins.
Ye who so many thousand kisses sung
Have read, deny male masculant I be?
You twain I'll —— and ——

## CATULLUS POUR HOMME INTENSE NO. 16

50ML EAU DE TOILETTE

The comeback of a flamboyant, intensely masculine scent, an assertive masculine seduction, as virile as it is sexy. A fragrance which offers a noncomformist view of masculinity. Sensual fresh haze of masculine salty caviar, warm honey and tart citrus fruits, bold enough to excite women, young men, even half-dead men. Leave envious friends speechless and sore with this scent's signature virility.

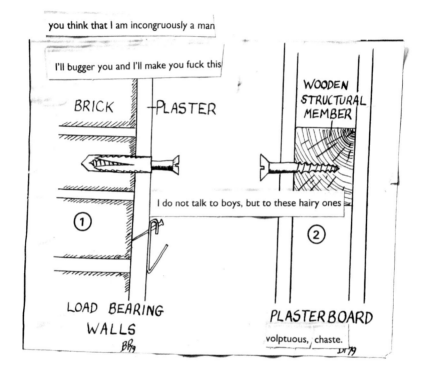

*Carmina Sutra*
*Position 16: The New Criticism*
*Richard O'Brien*

"The obs-
cenity of Catullus has long be-
en a stumbling block," writes
C. H. Sisson. 1 Carmen 16
probably offers more of
an impediment to the
translator than any o-
ther poem in the cor-
pus. An obvious *difficulty is*
in the repeated *first and final*
line. What can a translator *do with it? Un-*
til recently, Eng *lish as forth right as the Lat-*

| | |
|---|---|
| in could never | *be printed. Yet the poem* |
| — or rather a por | *tion of it — has been   a land-* |
| mark in literary | *criticism. The poem, as   trun-* |
| cated by the bo | *wdlerism of Cornish   and* |
| the athetism of | *Sisson, serves to allow   an* |
| innocent public to | *be ass   ured that Catullus* |
| was a fine Victorian | *gentle   man without prur-* |
| ient interests, a man | *proper   by our standards.* |
| Through not mak | *ing a   fair attempt to und-* |
| erstand the poem, | *Siss   on, a modern Proc-* |
| rustes, has replaced | *the "stumbling block" with* |
| a chopping block. | *— Thomas Nelson Winter.* |

## *Variations on Sexual Invective II*

*Assorted translations of the line 'Pedicabo ego vos et irrumabo':*

"I'll treat you as 'tis meet, I swear" (John Nott, 1795) / "I'll —— you twain and ——" (Sir Richard Francis Burton, 1894) / "I will paedicate and irrumate you" (Leonard C. Smithers, 1894) / "[omitted]" (Francis Warre-Cornish, 1904) / "Up your ass and in your mouth" (Carl Sesar, 1974) / "Fuck you, boys, up the butt and in the mouth" (Micaela Wakil Janan, 1994) / "Bugger off and get stuffed (...) as I bugger you both and stuff you up" (Josephine Balmer, 2004) / "The phrase threatens a violent sex act, the tribunal heard." (BBC News, 2009) "I'll push your shit in and stuff your face" (Carl Kohen, 2011) / "I'll sodomize and clintonize you" (Harry Walker, undated) / "I will sodomise and face-fuck you" (Wikisource, undated)

(How many can you work into friendly conversation over the span of a week? Keep score on this page.)

# XXI

AVRELI, pater esuritionum,

non harum modo, sed quot aut fuerunt

aut sunt aut aliis erunt in annis,

pedicare cupis meos amores.

Nec clam: nam simul es, iocaris una,

haerens ad latus omnia experiris.

Frustra: nam insidias mihi instruentemtangam

te prior irrumatione.

Atque id si faceres satur, tacerem:

nunc ipsum id doleo, quod esurire

me me puer et sitire discet.

Quare desine, dum licet pudico,

ne finem facias, sed irrumatus.

*1795/1894 mixed version*
*Leonard C. Smithers vs. John Nott*

Aurelius, father of the famished, in ages past, in time now present and in future years yet to come, thy lustful thoughts too freely rove. Nor is't done secretly: for to my charmer's side dost cling, trying every means. In vain dost impudently toy: for, instructed in thy artifice, I'll strike home beforehand. Now if thou didst this to work off the results of full-living, all this I'd bear: but what irks me is that my boy should learn to hunger, and to thirst. Wherefore, desist, whilst thou mayst with modesty. If not, I'll do a deed for thee.

*Aurelius: Nefariously*
*Harry Giles*

O, boss of throbs toto –
not long-lost solo comforts, who swoon off:
of comforts known now, comforts who grow, bloom, go forth –
who'd do sodom to GVC's consort, stop!
Not ghost words: Don John looks to lock
bottom to bottom from woos, coos, holds.
No-go, son: tho bold jocks sport,
hot-rod cock stops jock's gob.
Jock rocks off to porno or downtown dong? Cock holds off.
Mon horror: Don John cons GVC's boy to blowjob,
to bob on knob, slob schlong, wolf wood, bolt rod, slosh hog,
no know-how of tomorrow. So, coxcomb,
cordon off thon tool, fold on boy's good form,
or jock's topped off top down, both Os for cock to pop.

*Carmina Sutra*
*Position 21: The Pin*
Jon Stone

So
then,                          old
Aurelius,                   lord
of eternal        pantsfire,
you want a crack at my boy,
do you? Oh, I've seen
the two of you
horsing about,
the stray touch,
here, the flamey
look   there. Aye!
I see      you. One
step      over the
line,      Aurelius, *and it'll*
*be*          my      fat dyna*mite  stick*
*you're left*      hotly      suck*ing on.  Fair*
*exchange,  you*      might      ventur*e – oh,*
*for sure,*      *except that you're teachi*ng the *kid*
*to grow an appetite.* You're firin*g his thirst.* So d*on't,*
*OK? Back*      *off now,* with some dignity, or m*y half*
*pound*          'll be the *last thing*      you ever tas*te,*
*or*                  see.

*1970s Playboy ads version*
*Abi Palmer*

## *Alternative Testiomony*

Supposing you are the fought-over boy in the preceding poem. Draft your own missives, one to each of the older men. Will you choose a side? Reject both? Play them off against each other?

*Dear Catullus,*

*Dear Aurelius,*

# XXVI

FVRI, villula vestra non ad Austriflatus
opposita est neque ad Favoni
nec saevi Boreae aut Apheliotae,
verum ad milia quindecim et ducentos.
O ventum horribilem atque pestilentem!

*1795/1904 mixed version*
*John Nott vs. Francis Warre Cornish*

    To what wind, Furius,
does my little farm lie expos'd? –
Neither to the blasts of Auster the Southern gale,
nor Favonius the West,
nor fierce Boreas the Northern
or sunny-bosom'd Apheliotes,
but to a call
for fifteen thousand two hundred sesterces.
To that wind expos'd it lies ;
wind that brings horror,
wind of plagues!

*Furius: Anemiously*
*Harry Giles*

Fur's suburb hut's plush:
shuts up Uluru's gusts, spurns Duluth's puffs,
Lund's burst lungs, Kyushu's sussurus,
Such funds, Fur, such funds!
But such tumult, such scuds: rush rush rush.

# *A complaint*

Write to someone who is billing you. Protest your debt with a poem, or by namechecking several deities, or both at once. Stick the response in below.

# XXXII

AMABO, mea dulcis Ipsitilla,
meae deliciae, mei lepores,
iube ad te veniam meridiatum.
Et si iusseris, illud adiuvato,
ne quis liminis obseret tabellam,
neu tibi lubeat foras abire,
sed domi maneas paresque nobis
novem continuas fututiones.
Verum si quid ages, statim iubeto:
nam pransus iaceo et satur supinus
pertundo tunicamque palliumque.

❝ The speaker has no casual afternoon session planned, but rather it is a great favour he is slyly requesting (...) He is lying in bed, supine and erect, an epic warrior manqué, willingly and comically immobile. ❞

John R. Heath, *The Supine Hero in Catullus 32*

### Position 32: The She-Crab
*Jon Stone*

My dear
lady-sweet,
my darling
love-thing,
I ask you, I beg
you, call for me, make
it midday, and see your
way   to seeing that      no
one     else has drawn      the
bolt        on you, that      you
*your*      self are     not other-      wise
*occupied*     but, let's    say, suitable,  by which
*I mean to*     say suitably prepared for not one,
*not two,*       not three, not four, or five or six
*or even seven or*   eight but nine, oh yes,  nine
*tender, juicy, judicious*          bonings,  *and* now
*that I think of it, if you fancy it, there's no time* like
*the    present, since I've just finished eating, and* lie
*flat      on my back, ready to eat again, this*       great
*big serving spoon jutting out from my*         fat lap,
*keen to serve,   my sugardish.*

**1 Choose the right time.** Siesta sex is underrated ... and hot. Literally. Clear your diary for the afternoon.

**2 Leave the gate open.** Prepare the scene so that he can slip in without knocking.

**3 Dress (in)appropriately.** He already wants you. Drive him crazy with an outrageously revealing (and easily discardable) outfit.

**4 Don't forget to warm up.** Get your blood pumping before he arrives ... and we don't mean squat thrusts! (Though the odd knee lift isn't out of the question.)

**5 Don't let him off easily.** Remember, this is luncheon for two. You cleared your whole diary! So let him know that if he wants his favourite dish, he can stump up for another few courses, and lick the plate clean.

Yoooooooooooooooooo

You at yours?

Any1 else with you

I was thinking dinner, us 2

We could 'order in'? ;-D

I think I could go for like 9 'courses' ;-)))

tbh i just had dinner

But thinking about u always makes me hungry

You know im not talking about food right

### Sports Commentary Version
#### Andrea Tallerita

Now keep an eye on the number 11
this is bound to get good cause
she's got an eye on springing that offside trap.
Not sure how she'll make it past the line,
the centre's a bulldog, if she receives
that ball she and she does and look at
that I lost count of the stepovers
Now are you not entertained?
Say it: it's better than hogging the couch
unemployed and downloading porn.

### Ipsitilla's Reply
#### Gabrielle Nolan

Oh Catullus,
King of Romance...

Nine fucks,
such generosity!

But nine fucks
are ten too many.

Make use of that hole
in your tunic.

And leave mine alone.

## *An invitation*

Compose an invitation, requesting that someone you know indulge in something absolutely despicable. Address them by their full name. Copy it out, go to a bookshop and hide it in a book. Wait to see if it finds its way to the invitee.

# XL

QUAENAM te mala mens, miselle Ravide,
agit praecipitem in meos iambos?
Quis deus tibi non bene advocatus
vecordem parat excitare rixam?
An ut pervenias in ora vulgi?
Quid vis? Qualubet esse notus optas?
Eris, quandoquidem meos amores
cum longa voluisti amare poena.

*You Want Fame?*
*Claire Trévien*

Rime me this, Ravidus, you larval
poet: orange. It's not as hard as
ripe typers claim. Come, your carnival
brain should wrap around it quickish.
Ribbed with victory, your retrieval
will be less unwelcome than those
risible efforts to troll me, rival
only in your head. Call yourself a poet?
Rise to the occasion then, you disapproval-
addict, here's a few: lozenge, or goldfinch in the
right accent will do, shape your mouth oval
like and wait for the wind to change.

## Shade to throw

Use this page to collect your favourite put-downs. Deploy them sparingly!

# XLVIII

MELLITOS oculos tuos, Iuventi,
si quis me sinat usque basiare,
usque ad milia basiem trecenta
nec numquam videar satur futurus,
non si densior aridis aristis
sit nostrae seges osculationis.

*1795 / 1894 hybrid version*
*John Nott vs. Richard Francis Burton*

TO HIS FAVOURITE

FREELY were I allow'd to kiss
Those honied eyes of thine (Juventius!)
If any suffer me sans stint to buss,
No numbers would complete my bliss,
Not show'rs of kisses would suffice:
I'd kiss of kisses hundred thousands three,
Nor ever deem I'd reach satiety,
Though richer harvests of each kiss were born
The kissing harvests richest sun-burnt
field of kiss of kisses show'rs honied numbers
wheat-ears corn kisses (!)

*Juventius: Euphorically*
*Harry Giles*


If kid bid I kiss his kirsch lids –
kiss him I, II, III; bis bis –
I'd kiss his prisms in CCC shifts.
This thirst, this itch, isn't dimming,
vivid still if the kiss-kiss-kissing
is rich till mills fill in innings.




*Juventius' Reply*
*Gabrielle Nolan*

Poor poppet.
Yes, I understand
so many kisses
wouldn't satisfy
either of our hungers.
You must kiss me lower,

lower, lower, down –
yes – and an ear of corn

would be a welcome addition
to your tongue's wet work.

*Carmina Sutra*
*Position 48: The Limpet*
*Jon Stone*


Voo
ventuth,
if only
I cooth
kith your
honeyith
eyeth with
out pawth,
thyit, I'd
kithem
THREE *HUN*
D RERD *THOUTH*
*A* ND TIM *ETH*
*at* leatht, *and*
*eve*n then I'd *be*
*only jutht getting*
thtart*ed. Thyit,*
I woul*dn't be*
finithed *even if*
the mat*hed heap*
of thtill *thmoking*
kith eth *outclathed*
thu m *mathith*
har *vetht of*
cro*pth, do you*
hear me, *Vooventuth? I'd jutht*
go right *on kith-kith-kithing.*

## *Portrait of the Receiver of Kisses*

Recite a version of this poem to a friend or stranger, and live-sketch their reaction below.

# L

Hesterno, Licini, die otiosi
multum lusimus in meis tabellis,
ut convenerat esse delicatos:
scribens versiculos uterque nostrum
ludebat numero modo hoc modo illoc,
reddens mutua per iocum atque vinum.
Atque illinc abii tuo lepore
incensus, Licini, facetiisque,
ut nec me miserum cibus iuvaret
nec somnus tegeret quiete ocellos,
sed toto indomitus furore lecto
versarer, cupiens videre lucem,
ut tecum loquerer simulque ut essem.
At defessa labore membra postquam
semimortua lectulo iacebant,
hoc, iucunde, tibi poema feci,
ex quo perspiceres meum dolorem.
Nunc audax cave sis, precesque nostras,
oramus, cave despuas, ocelle,
ne poenas Nemesis reposcat a te.
Est vemens dea: laedere hanc caveto.

O Licinius, we at leisure have played
many things on my boards,
as we agreed to be racy:

█████████████████████
███████████████████████████
█████████████████████████████
████████████████████████
██████████████████████████████

████ as a result neither food helps my misery
nor sleep quietly covers my eyes,
but untamed I as a result might turn with total fury,
desiring to see the light,
so that I might speak with you at the same time I might be
with you.

█████████████████████████████
███████████████████
██████████████████████████
███████████████████
████████████████████
██████████████████████████
██████████████████████
█████████████████████████████████

*'Friendship': party game version*
*Kirsten Irving*

*For 2 players*

*You will need:*
pens, to write together; wine, to drink together; uneaten food; a delightful jewel; Nemesis kit, comprising a measuring rod, bridle, scales, sword and scourge.

*Aim:*
To be close, to keep counters nearby, to share the days. To end at sunset, so close your arm hairs interlock.

*Instructions:*
Each player takes a turn to move toward the other, then draws a By Jove! card. By Jove! cards introduce Awkward points; to avoid a Scandal, players with 5 points must move apart by the spaces shown or invent a reason and pray it's accepted. If a reason holds water, the excusee breathes out and draws a Risk card.

*Risk cards include:*
- **Sleepless Nights**. Collect three of these and blurt out half-awake praise to your friend. 2 Awkward.
- **Thrown Together**. If you get this card too soon, 2 Awkward.
- **Worn Limbs**. Distraction, wasting, a person can be fatal. 2 Awkward. Always 2 Awkward.

*Ending:*
If both players reach sunset in each other's arms, gain Unending Fidelity, and both win.

**WARNING**: If a player accrues 10 Awkward points, they anger Nemesis. There is no remedy. The Nemesis Kit descends upon them in full hot blood, they are measured and whipped, and everything ends.

## *Your turn*

Invent a short game to be played between you and a friend.

# LI

Ille mi par esse deo videtur,
ille, si fas est, superare divos,
qui sedens adversus identidem te
    spectat et audit
dulce ridentem, misero quod omnes
eripit sensus mihi: nam simul te,
Lesbia, aspexi, nihil est super mi
    vocis in ore;
lingua sed torpet, tenuis sub artus
flamma demanat, sonitu suopte
tintinant aures, gemina teguntur
    lumina nocte.
otium, Catulle, tibi molestum est:
otio exsultas nimiumque gestis:
otium et reges prius et beatas
    perdidit urbes.

Catullus 51 is an imitation of a fragment by Sappho, written over 500 years prior:

*Sappho 31 (Aeolic Greek)*

φαίνεταί μοι κῆνος ἴσος θέοισιν
ἔμμεν᾽ ὤνηρ, ὄττις ἐνάντιός τοι
ἰσδάνει καὶ πλάσιον ἆδυ φωνεί-
    σας ὑπακούει

καὶ γελαίσας ἰμέροεν, τό μ᾽ ἦ μὰν
καρδίαν ἐν στήθεσιν ἐπτόαισεν·
ὠς γὰρ ἔς σ᾽ ἴδω βρόχε᾽, ὤς με φώναι-
    σ᾽ οὐδ᾽ ἓν ἔτ᾽ εἴκει,

ἀλλ᾽ ἄκαν μὲν γλῶσσα †ἔαγε†, λέπτον
δ᾽ αὔτικα χρῶι πῦρ ὑπαδεδρόμηκεν,
ὀππάτεσσι δ᾽ οὐδ᾽ ἓν ὄρημμ᾽, ἐπιρρόμ-
    βεισι δ᾽ ἄκουαι,

†έκαδε μ᾽ ἴδρως ψῦχρος κακχέεται†, τρόμος δὲ
παῖσαν ἄγρει, χλωροτέρα δὲ ποίας
ἔμμι, τεθνάκην δ᾽ ὀλίγω ᾽πιδεύης
    φαίνομ᾽ ἔμ᾽ αὔται·
ἀλλὰ πὰν τόλματον ἐπεὶ †καὶ πένητα†

---

*Translation of the above by Henry Thornton Wharton, 1885*

That man seems to me peer of gods, who sits in thy presence, and hears close to him thy sweet speech and lovely laughter; that indeed makes my heart flutter in my bosom. For when I see but a little, I have no utterance left, my tongue is broken down, and straightaway a subtle fire has run under my skin, with my eyes I have no sight, my ears ring, sweat bathes me, and a trembling seizes all my body; I am paler than grass, and seem in my madness little better than dead. But I must dare all, since one so poor ...

Him rival to the gods I place,
  Him loftier yet, if loftier be,
Who, Lesbia, sits before thy face,
  Who listens and who looks on thee;

Thee smiling soft. Yet this delight
  Doth all my sense consign to death;
For when thou dawnest on my sight,
  Ah, wretched! flits my labouring breath.

My tongue is palsied. Subtly hid
  Fire creeps me through from limb to limb:
My loud ears tingle all unbid:
  Twin clouds of night mine eyes bedim.

Ease is my plague: ease makes thee void,
  Catullus, with these vacant hours,
And wanton: ease that hath destroyed
  Great kings, and states with all their powers.

*Following pages: versions of 51 in six pulp genres*

**EPISODE LI.**

*The God Emperor has achieved ultimate power. Throned in Lesbia's laughter, he commands the known galaxy.*

*Meanwhile, in the darkest reaches of the Umbral Cloud, the crew of the Catullus prepare to crash-land on a nearby dwarf planet. With their engines on fire, their comms shot and their sensors offline, survival seems unlikely.*

*Languishing in skeletal outposts, slow to retaliate, the Resistance now stands poised on the brink of lasting defeat ...*

hat guy is probably a werewolf. Just saying.
That mortal, if indeed he be, more immortal
        than even me,
who sits by you in Double Chem,
        staring hungrily,
his ears coned

to your laughter (which belongs to me,
anaesthetises me). Nothing matters
when I look at you, Lesbia; I mutter your name
then stalk off, silenced by my burden.

My tongue is addicted to you; white heat
fills my cold, ripped body; your milkshake
my heroin. I pull on shades
and plan your kidnap in the darkened gym.

Blood, Catullus, will ruin this date.
Blood will bring out the monster you were.
Blood makes you break into bedrooms, and y'know,
most girls don't go for that anymore.

# "FIFTY-ONE"

Lesbia, smoking hot in shifting satin,
a red Schiaparelli number, cut-to-kill,
spaghetti strap artfully loose on one bare
white arm. Her hooks tonight are in
millionaire Crassus. He's slavering,
luckiest grifter in Little Italy, Straight Flush,
Full House, Jack in the Hole. Rufus,
I tell the barman, hit me with another.
Lesbia. She was Clodia back then.
The shock when she walked through
my door. Like the sizzle that twitched
Antonius. I wired him up to the factory mains.
He went pasty, his legs shook, sawdust-mouthed,
he fizzed inside, talked, and blacked out.
Catullus, I tell myself, here's the angle:
trouble comes when there's time to burn.
Time on your hands, Christ, you're an animal.
Flagrant time. It's what got Philoctetes
the Greek wasted. It did for Babylon.

# Death Carries A Parasol

Ah, this again: the beach break. G. should have known
that's how Rome fell; too many senator siestas.
Nonetheless, here he was with a woman to forget
and a pension bed, with a window onto –

what else? – the sea. Most inconveniently,
the sea of mystery, just then, threw up
a gent in a Homburg hat, his arm
linked in the crook of another, leading to…

a face he thought he'd left behind in Paultons Square.
G. leapt. What was he do to but follow?
For he had been followed, and comprehensively.
Hearing the old laugh, seeing the old smile

as if replayed through a souped-up gramophone,
directed not at himself, but at him…
This must be how it felt to a Greek
ploughing the turf at the foot of Mount Olympus,

to look up at those surly chieftains,
those gilded thugs who called themselves
the Gods: a position surely rightly reserved
for the man now rounding the corner

in his Homburg with the woman
G. had come to – was she going willingly?
That laugh, now he considered it, had the ring of desperation –
a kidnapper and his hostage on the move.

Now, at a goodly clip, he trailed them,
sticking close as a gecko. Something had to be said,
and yet, how dare he speak to her?
It seemed the most impossible temerity,

though not, admittedly, as bold
as bringing a married woman to the Costa.
He sought opportunities for interruption:
an urn to unbalance, a fisherman to bribe.

He lost them down an alley, and another alley.
Dusk tinged the harbour – the locals
fussed with wicker chairs and awnings.
Their weather-beaten faces seemed to hint

that there was no great mystery
other than getting to the end of the day.
On reflection: had it really been her?
All he'd had to go on was the drift of a shawl.

Yet a man might keep a gun under his Homburg.
Why else should he keep it on, in this weather?
A hat with a pin gleaming in the hatband:
a pin last seen in – think, G., think! –

the most notorious murder of the century.
Stuck in the heart of a Duke like a cocktail umbrella.
G. considered the novel he was reading
and dearly wanted to be bought an ice.

He couldn't now. Away with idleness!
He could strike again. There wasn't a moment to lose.

CHAPTER 51

IN THE tavern, they sat near the fire, which created a
companionate halo around the small company. Food was
served, with ale and mead, and they started to feel merry,
though tired and shaken by the terrors of the road. Snorri was
elbow height to the rider in the green cloak, whose pitted face
now seemed moon-like, lit by the elf woman who sat opposite,
talking and smiling. Her laughter was like purses of silver poured
out liberally and pocketed by that mortal. None of it was spent
on the dwarf, who sat in shadow and twice looked at her and
quickly turned away as he felt flames dart along his limbs. He
tried once to speak, but his tongue was lead and he knew he could
not speak and look at her still. His senses eclipsed, he heard only
the pounding on the worn anvil of his heart. His eyes were shut
in darkness, like the closing of the doors into the mountain.
Confused by these new emotions, he applied himself with greater
energy to the meal. Idleness, thought Snorri, taking great bites of
the bread and roast meat in his trencher. Only idleness. The idle
axe rusts and the lazy smith lets his fire go out.

# STRANGER WITH NO NAME

he kicked open those ol' swing doors,
framed by the sun in a way
which occured to me later coulda been
utterly godlike (coulda been the devil),

there was a glint in his eye that spoke louder
than those other wanderers, and I seen all sorts
(moonshine-hungry bastards).

he sat right here, I tell you,
and stared, colt-straight, into the face
of One-Click Johnny. never batted an eye,

not at the midnight women who tried
to pry him upstairs away from the booze,
not even as Johnny laughed with his goons
in a manner that wrangles my cold insides.

coulda been war. but at that same time,
and maybe it was an act of god (maybe the devil),
Lesbia (that unattainable whore) begins to dance.

I dont dare speak. my tongue is sand.
a cactus-prick rises and falls on the spot
where i stand. the clapped-out piano rings
that same ol' honky-tonk tune. what is it?
a whisper? a warning? a love song. naw,

git me the hell outta here,

I spit into two shining glasses. no one moves,
all eyes point to bustles and flounces. I pour

and keep on wiping,
but there ain't much work for these fingers
and thumbs no more.

I tell myself, Catullus, you'se seen
this trouble before –
weapons drawn before noon,

time to face the horizon and walk:
a heart as old and itching
as mine can get crotchety,

Catullus knows
idle hands have burned barns into dust,
turned desert sands into empty  railroads

## 51.

Pick another writer. Compose a version of this poem in their style.

# LVI

O REM ridiculam, Cato, et iocosam,
dignamque auribus et tuo cachinno!
ride quidquid amas, Cato, Catullum:
res est ridicula et nimis iocosa.
deprendi modo pupulum puellae
trusantem; hunc ego, si placet Dionae,
protelo rigida mea cecidi.


*In six words:*

Boy jackhammers girl. Catullus hijacks boy.


*1894 / 1894 / 1904 hybrid version*
*Leonard C. Smithers vs. Richard Francis Burton vs. John Nott*

O risible matter (Cato!) and jocose,
and worthy of thine ears and thy laughter.
Just now I caught a boy, a young blade
attempting to rifle a lass,
and on him, sweet Venus,
with stiffest staff I fell.

# *Fresco*

Scene from the wall of the Suburban Baths at Pompeii. Embellish this with further details.

# LXV

Etsi me assiduo confectum cura dolore
sevocat a doctis, Ortale, virginibus,
nec potis est dulcis Musarum expromere fetus
mens animi, tantis fluctuat ipsa malis--
namque mei nuper Lethaeo in gurgite fratris
pallidulum manans alluit unda pedem,
Troia Rhoeteo quem subter litore tellus
ereptum nostris obterit ex oculis.
. . . . . . . .
numquam ego te, vita frater amabilior,
aspiciam posthac? at certe semper amabo,
semper maesta tua carmina morte canam,
qualia sub densis ramorum concinit umbris
Daulias, absumpti fata gemens Ityli--
sed tamen in tantis maeroribus, Ortale, mitto
haec expressa tibi carmina Battiadae,
ne tua dicta vagis nequiquam credita ventis
effluxisse meo forte putes animo,
ut missum sponsi furtivo munere malum
procurrit casto virginis e gremio,
quod miserae oblitae molli sub veste locatum,
dum adventu matris prosilit, excutitur,
atque illud prono praeceps agitur decursu,
huic manat tristi conscius ore rubor.

*You Asked Catullus...*
*Tim Dooley*


You asked
Catullus for a poem
hoping, I suppose
for something
FRUITY
with the SLAP
of FLESH and TICKLE of
his wit. He disappoints.
His mind is with that
round-faced friend who
disappeared last summer,
leaving only his laughing
voice behind.
Well... since
you asked, here's a
translation from a long-dead
poet. Think of it as like that apple
the lover picked and gave to the girl
who hid it under her dress, the cold
fruit skin like a secret kiss against her
skin. Think of the blush on the girl's face
as, hearing her mother at the door, she
stood up in a guilty rush
letting the fruit
fall
rolling slowly
along the wooden floor.

## *Brothers*
### *Kirsten Irving*

*(an assemblage version, made from Rilke's 'Letters to a Young Poet #7'*
*(as translated bt Stephen Mitchell) and Elton John's 'Daniel')*


Much time has passed since I received your last letter. Daniel
is a star in the face of the sky. Please don't hold that against me;
first it was work, then a number of interruptions, and I can see
the red tail lights heading for Spain; poor health
that again and again kept me from answering. Oh and I can see
Daniel waving goodbye. I wanted my answer to come to you
out of peaceful and happy days. (God it looks like Daniel,
must be the clouds in my eyes.) Now I feel somewhat better again
You see: I have copied out your sonnet (They say Spain is pretty
though I've never been) because I found that it is lovely and simple.
Daniel says it's the best and born in the shape that it moves in
with such quiet decorum. Oh and he should know,
he's been there enough. And now I am giving you this copy
because I know that it is important (Lord I miss Daniel)
and full of new experience to rediscover a work of one's own
(oh, I miss him so much) in someone else's handwriting.

## *An appropriation*

Write whatever you like, but put on the TV or radio or a podcast or audiobook while you do. Integrate phrases and images from the broadcast as you write.

# LXXII

Dicebas quondam solum te nosse Catullum,
Lesbia, nec prae me velle tenere Iouem.
dilexi tum te non tantum ut vulgus amicam,
sed pater ut gnatos diligit et generos.
nunc te cognovi: quare etsi impensius uror,
multo mi tamen es vilior et levior.
qui potis est, inquis? quod amantem iniuria talis
cogit amare magis, sed bene velle minus.

❝ In order to clarify what his feelings are, he
carefully organises a series of contrasts
between carnal and romantic love [that]
reveal in full the greatest issue of his life in
eight short lines. ❞

John T. Davies, *Poetic Counterpoint: Catullus 72*

*Carmina Sutra*
*Position 72: The Shoveller*
*Jon Stone*

You
used to
love me
harder
than
anything.
Fuck Jove;
Catullus
was your
guy. And
me, well,
*what* I felt for
you *was as* deep
as *the love a* father
*feels for his sons* – not
*mere*      *fanboyism. Now I know* you,
*and the hotter it gets, the more* of *a sham*
*you seem. Sorry? How come?*   Well, *when*       you
*thoroughly crush a person the*   way *you* crushed me, it makes
*them want you*       all the *more … but like you all the less.*

## Lesbia's Reply
### Ian McLachlan

So I said a few things to get my leg over,
guff about picking you instead of Jove.
Passion thrives on a skilful tongue –
your words, I believe. We had a riot.
Then you slap me with this sour outburst.
You loved me, you claim, as a father does
his sons and sons-in-law. Lucky me.
Explains your fondness for anal.
You should have stuck with Alfenus.
Or Juventius. Never stopped greasing it
with Syrian oil for them, did you, lover?
How is your little willy by the way?
Not as cobwebby as your purse, I hope.
Dinner at my expense every time and you
call me cheap. Want to know why I cooled?
It was the sex. You preferred it like your poems,
short. Egnatius keeps me hot for several hours.
And he gets in the Falernian. So let it go,
Catullus. I did love you. Like I loved my
sparrow. What more can I say, pet?

## *A looting*

Rifle the original Latin for English words (or anagrams of English words), and then make something new from them:

        mad   mute          mull

DICEBAS quondam solum te nosse Catullum,

# LXXV

Hvc est mens deducta tua mea, Lesbia, culpa
atque ita se officio perdidit ipsa suo,
ut iam nec bene velle queat tibi, si optima fias,
nec desistere amare, omnia si facias.

▼

*Latin into English*
*Tiffany Anne Tondut*

Here's the thing - you've done me in, dirty Lesbia,
and yet I've fucked myself by serving hell,
so I cannot wish you well, should you reach your premium,
or give up loving, if all you're worth is nil.

▼

*English into Indonesian*
*Kate Wakeling*

Ada satu hal – Lesbia sudah membuat aku tergila-gila,
meskipun aku akan mengakui itu terkutuk itu sendiri dengan mencintaimu
aku tahu aku tidak bisa berharap kamu dengan baik, jika kamu mencapai
  puncakmu,
atau menyerah mencintai, jika semua yang kamu nilai adalah nol.

▼

*Indonesian back into English*
*via Google Translate*

There is one thing – Lesbia has made me crazy,
Though I will admit it is damned itself by loving you

I know I can not expect you well, if you reach your peak,
Or give up loving, if all you value is zero.

▼

### English into German
*Kirsten Irving and Inga Vesper*

Es gibt etwas anderes – Lesbia hat mir zum Wahsinn getrieben
obwohl ich zugeben muss, dass alles verdammt ist, wenn es dich liebt.
Ich weiss, dass ich allenfalls nichts von dir erwarten kann,
und wenn du nichts bewertest, soll ich die Liebe aufgeben.

▼

### German back into English
*Jon Stone*

There's something more – Lesbia has broken my mind,
though I must say: all who love you are equally damned!
Nothing, nothing at all for me while you rule the roost,
and I cannot love you if you value nothing.

▼

### English into simplified Chinese
*Jennifer Wong*

还有的是，里斯比亚已搅扰了我的思想。
然而我必须说的是，爱你的人也是同受罪的！
当你是我的统治者，我自己什么也不能驾驭。
如果你不先珍惜我，我也无法去爱你。

▼

There is also that Lesbia has disturbed my thoughts.
But what I have to say is that those who love you are also guilty!
When you are my ruler, I can not control anything myself.
If you do not cherish me first, I can not love you too.

▼

*English into Romanesco*
*Andrea Tallarita*

E sai che c'é? Che Lesbia m'ha scombussolato 'a zucca.
Epperó, 'na cosa: che chi te vo' bene anche rui c'ha corpa.
Quanno me governi, 'n posso piú controllá gnente.
Se te 'n me voi bene, 'n te poss'amá manch'io.

▼

*Romanesco back into English*
*via Google Translate*

And you know what it is? That Lesbia has squandered me like pumpkin.
Yep, what it is, is: you who are good also have the body.
That's my government, I've got more control over you.
If you do me well, I can have you without me.

*Lesbia's Reply*
*Craig Dobson*

Listen, devotee, you couldn't score
whether I was best girl or whore.
Just keep loving and writing me more.
All's fair, if hard, in love and war.

## *Future archaeology*

Transcribe some toilet block graffiti. Take it home and translate it into Latin. Now re-graffiti it somewhere else. Bonus points if the subject is romance.

# LXXXI

Nemone in tanto potuit populo esse, Iuventi,
bellus homo, quem tu diligere inciperes.
praeterquam iste tuus moribunda ab sede Pisauri
hospes inavrata palladior statua,
qui tibi nunc cordi est, quem tu praeponere nobis
audes, et nescis quod facinus facias?


### Juventius: Equivocally
#### Harry Giles

There teem men he'd best prefer!
Pet needs the sweet defender, yet selects
the dreck: the wretch dwells where the tenement hell
resembles feeble pewter, where excellence peters.
Pet's tenderness bedecks the plebe; pet deserts me,
yet pretends he's deed-free. Pet's senseless.


### Juventius' Reply
#### Gabrielle Nolan

You are the last that should complain
of my 'strange taste.'

My heart, and cock, always weep
for the least fortunate.

## _____ *versus John Nott*

Complete this version however you like.


TO HIS FAVOURITE


CAN none, of all the Roman race,

　　Engage your

　　　　　in your fond embrace




That wretch, whom you so much prefer,

　　Is

But, o sweet

　　　　　whom you trust.

# LXXXIII

Lesbia mi praesente viro mala plurima dicit:
haec illi fatuo maxima laetitia est.
mule, nihil sentis? si nostri oblita taceret,
sana esset: nunc quod gannit et obloquitur,
non solum meminit, sed, quae multo acrior est res,
irata est. hoc est, uritur et loquitur.

*1894/1894/1904 mixed version*
*Richard Francis Burton vs. Leonard C. Smithers vs. Francis Warre Cornish*

Lesbia heaps upon me foul words in the presence of her husband, a great joy to that ninny. Mule! You understand nothing. If she forgot us in silence, she would be heart-whole. But now whatso she rails and she snarls and scolds: not only does she remember, but — a much more serious, bitterer thing — she is enraged; she is afire and she fumes and ripens her passion all the while she is talking.

### Lesbia's Reply
*Gabrielle Nolan*

Oh, Catullus
How clever you are
You know a woman's mind as well
as you know the wishbone of her clit
That is
not even a bit!

## Carmina says:

Write an advice column.

# LXXXV

Odi et amo. Quare id faciam, fortasse requiris.
nescio, sed fieri sentio et excrucior.

*1904 version*
*Francis Warre Cornish*

I hate and love. Why I do so, perhaps you ask. I know
not, but I feel it, and I am in torment.

*Variations on the first line*
*Many translators*

Hate I, and love I, I hate and I love, THO' I hate, yet
I love ! I hate, and yet I love thee too, I LOVE and
I HATE, O th'hate and I move love, I hate her and I
love her, I hate and love her.

Perhaps you wonder why. Wherefore would I do this,
perhaps you ask? Haps thou'lt ask me wherefore
I do so. Wherefore do I so, peradventure thou askest.
You'll perhaps ask me, how? You may ask why I do so.
You ask, "How can this be?" Quarry it fact I am, for
that's so re queries. Don't ask me why – wherefore
I cannot tell. Ah! Never ask why so!

*Mixtape version*
Abigail Parry

Tattoo version
Abigail Parry

# Columns

Be on the look out for other odd couples and unlikely pairings, down in the pits of your heart or elsewhere. Record them here.

# XCIX

SVRRIPVI tibi, dum ludis, mellite Iuventi,
suaviolum dulci dulcius ambrosia.
verum id non impune tuli: namque amplius horam
suffixum in summa me memini esse cruce,
dum tibi me purgo nec possum fletibus ullis
tantillum vestrae demere saevitiae.
nam simul id factum est, multis diluta labella
guttis abstersisti omnibus articulis,
ne quicquam nostro contractum ex ore maneret,
tamquam commictae spurca saliva lupae.
praeterea infesto miserum me tradere amori
non cessasti omnique excruciare modo,
ut mi ex ambrosia mutatum iam foret illud
suaviolum tristi tristius elleboro.
quam quoniam poenam misero proponis amori,
numquam iam posthac basia surripiam.

*In six words:*

I ain't some good-for-nothing floozy, Juvy.

I stole from thee, whilst thou wert fucking,
     sticky faced Iackie,
   a sweeter kiss than sweet sambuca,
     somewhere puckerd.
  But things got messy. I myself got naild
     for a hard & sweaty hour, said Im sorry
  & burst into tears, but thou kept pushing.
     When it was done, thou tookst the wet
  bukake skein of loue from eies, lips, cheek.
     & wipst them with thy fingers
  as if a iunkie tom had gobbd it there
     & then thou toldst me about thy diagnosis,
  fart & heldst my head beneath the couers,
       tweetest my name with a pic of a little finger –
  so now I think, I put my tongue up where?
       & the tyte wont go howeuer I brush my teeth.
  Do as ye would be done by: the uicars prouerb

     rings suddenly true now Iue been sóffS.

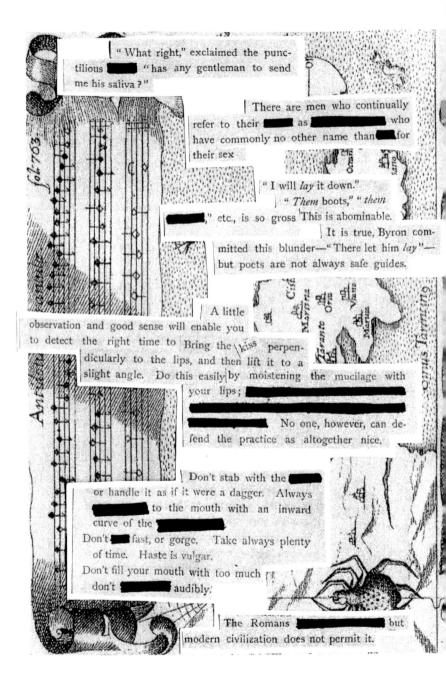

"What right," exclaimed the punctilious ██████ "has any gentleman to send me his saliva?"

There are men who continually refer to their ████ as ████████ who have commonly no other name than ██ for their sex

"I will *lay* it down."
"*Them* boots," "*them* ████████," etc., is so gross This is abominable. It is true, Byron committed this blunder—"There let him *lay*"—but poets are not always safe guides.

A little observation and good sense will enable you to detect the right time to Bring the kiss perpendicularly to the lips, and then lift it to a slight angle. Do this easily by moistening the mucilage with your lips; ████████████████ ████████████ No one, however, can defend the practice as altogether nice.

Don't stab with the ████ or handle it as if it were a dagger. Always ████████████ to the mouth with an inward curve of the ████████ Don't ████ fast, or gorge. Take always plenty of time. Haste is vulgar. Don't fill your mouth with too much ████ don't ████████ audibly:

The Romans ████████████ but modern civilization does not permit it.

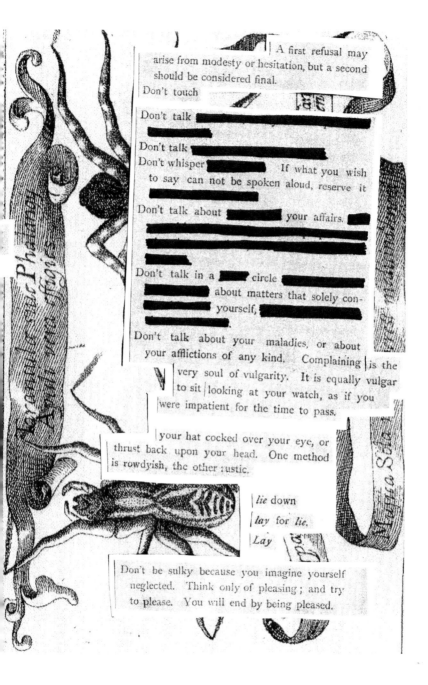

A first refusal may arise from modesty or hesitation, but a second should be considered final.

Don't touch

Don't talk ████████

Don't talk ████

Don't whisper ██████ If what you wish to say can not be spoken aloud, reserve it

Don't talk about ██████ your affairs. ██████

Don't talk in a ████ circle ██████ about matters that solely con- ████ yourself, ██████

Don't talk about your maladies, or about your afflictions of any kind. Complaining is the very soul of vulgarity. It is equally vulgar to sit looking at your watch, as if you were impatient for the time to pass.

your hat cocked over your eye, or thrust back upon your head. One method is rowdyish, the other rustic.

*lie* down
*lay* for *lie*.
*Lay*

Don't be sulky because you imagine yourself neglected. Think only of pleasing; and try to please. You will end by being pleased.

A stolen kiss. A honey-sweet boy.

Can he get away with it?

Latin playboy Catullus is in love – and agony – after making out with dreamy young noble Juventius. Juventius insists it was a mistake and tries to cover up the incident, blanking Catullus at social gatherings. Catullus is heartbroken, angry at being treated like a dirty secret, but if anything, Juventius' dismissiveness makes the swaggering youth all the more desirable. Can Catullus save himself further pain? Or will he be unable to resist those ambrosia lips a second time?

**" And so it would seem that those who truly have foul mouths do well, while the poet, whose mouth is not really foul at all, gets nowhere with Juventius. "**

Phyllis Young Forsyth, *Order and Meaning in Catullus 97-99*

 **Version**

Produce your own adaptation, revision or reimagining of this poem, then reward yourself with a 99 flake.

# CI

Mvltas per gentes et multa per aequora vectus
advenio has miseras, frater, ad inferias,
ut te postremo donarem munere mortis
et mutam nequiquam alloquerer cinerem.
Quandoquidem fortuna mihi tete abstulit ipsum.
Heu miser indigne frater adempte mihi,
nunc tamen interea haec, prisco quae more parentum
tradita sunt tristi munere ad inferias,
accipe fraterno multum manantia fletu,
atque in perpetuum, frater, ave atque vale.


### 101
*Jei Degenhardt*

Many bodies. Many flat oceans. I've been moving
, arriving's misery. Brother. Funeral.
Last things for you, dead
and silence speaking with ashes
since we're taken from me. Luck.
Wrong. How you're gone. Brother. From me.

, now. Blink. Something old, last time
again passed, living to dead. Please.
Take, like breath. offering drops damp
and always. Brother. turn and

Write a letter to someone you miss.

# CXVI

Saepe tibi studioso animo venante requirens
carmina uti possem mittere Battiadae,
qui te lenirem nobis, neu conarere
tela infesta meum mittere in usque caput,
hunc uideo mihi nunc frustra sumptum esse laborem,
Gelli, nec nostras hic ualuisse preces.
contra nos tela ista tua evitabimus amitha
at fixus nostris tu dabis supplicium.

*1904/1973 hybrid version*
*Francis Warre Cornish vs. C.W. MacLeod's critical essay* Catullus 116

I would have liked to send you such-and-such a kind of poem, Gellius.
I have cast about with busy questing mind how I could work in
reconciliation, erudition and polish, that you might not send a shower
of missiles to reach my head. But my prayers have here availed nothing.
I can only send you this un-Callimachean inverted dedication, rich in
invective. I parry those uncouth missiles of yours by wrapping my cloak
round my arm; but you shall be pierced and punished by the irresistible
power of vituperation. Farewell!

*Loosed arrows version*
Erik Kennedy

Lately,
I've hunted in my studious brain,
inquired
of it:
how do I make myself attractive to Gellius?
I've

put on
(figurative) wigs, sent Callimachus-style greeting-
cards,
and
generally sexed myself and my poems up
five-

fold.
One parcel I mailed came limping
back

with
an arrow cleanly through it. I suppose you're
tired

of all
this, my stertorous, heaving love and the poems.
Fuck.

The
brain now writes poems like this one,
hard

shots
at war, as if it were a spittoon. I'm ready to explode and
flail,

eh, Gellius,
eh? I'm prepared: a starched shirt is the virtuous man's armour. Open
your mail.

# CXVII

T.P. Wiseman says: "It is tempting to suppose that [Catullus 116] is a spurious addition, attached after the publication of the collection". Attach your own spurious addition below by falsifying the long-lost 117th poem of Catullus. Bonus points for writing in Latin.

## 2. CATULLUS

**remixed, reparcelled,
refitted, ripped off,
riffed off, revived,
rummaged in,
rifled through,
ribbed and rekindled.**

QVOMODO · EQVO · TROIANO.
SIMILIS · LESBIA?
INTRA · EAM · QVOQVE ·
EXERCITVS · HOMINVM · FVIT

Unctis falciferi senis diebus,
regnator quibus inperat fritillus,
versu ludere non laborioso
permittis, puto, pilleata Roma.
Risisti; licet ergo, non vetamur.
Pallentes procul hinc abite curae;
quidquid venerit obvium loquamur
morosa sine cogitatione.
Misce dimidios, puer, trientes,
quales Pythagoras dabat Neroni,
misce, Dindyme, sed frequentiores:
possum nil ego sobrius; bibenti
succurrent mihi quindecim poetae.
Da nunc basia, sed Catulliana:
quae si tot fuerint quot ille dixit,
donabo tibi Passerem Catulli.

*Translation of the above from Bohn's Classical Library (1897):*

In these festive days of the scythe-bearing old man, when the dice-box rules supreme, you will permit me, I feel assured, cap-clad Rome, to sport in unlaboured verse. You smile: I may do so then, and am not forbidden. Depart, pale cares, far away from hence; let us say whatever comes uppermost without disagreeable reflection. Mix cup after cup, my attendants, such as Pythagoras used to give to Nero; mix, Dindymus, mix still faster. I can do nothing without wine; but, while I am drinking, the power of fifteen poets will show itself in me. Now give me kisses, such as Catullus would have loved; and if I receive as many as he describes, I will give you the sparrow of Catullus.

*Catullus' Agony*
*Harry Giles*

*Kathleen Latham*

**I am all ear**

> **my love,**
> **cocked to the rhythm**
> **of your**          silkgloved
>                    **voice**, rocked in the
> sway                    of your slow-
>           tongued song  – I am a shell
>                on your  sounding
>           stream          bound for

> **that-wild-and-**
> **witching-**
> **sea**

*("You will ask the gods, O Fabullus, to make you all nose"* – Catullus 13)

To whom
should I present
this little book?

The sour-faced
strictures of the wise

What a woman
tells her lover
in desire

Your rival has gout

Do stop smiling,
Egnatius

You've a wild goat
under your armpits,
Rufus

Calvus - *what*
have I done to deserve
so many poets?

Just good old
Falernian,
and lots of it.

Every time I see her

Asinius,
napkin-snatcher

Try the bridge,
my Veronese friend

Remember the radish,
Aurelius

Suffenus,
touched by the Muses

I've found somewhere
to keep your annals,
Volusius

Ravidus, impaled
on my iambics

Lesbia is extraordinarily
vindictive about me
in front of her husband

Your mouth,
Aemilius

**Furius! Aurelius!**

The passing plough

The radish, Aurelius

Your sparrow,
Darling

*Home truths*
*Lindsay MacGregor*

Less of the         -talk, Catullus! Lesbia

is unimpressed by boys whose prowess doesn't

        up to all their claims. And, frankly, much

of what you write is        . Your million bitter

kisses leave her cold. She prefers the sweeter

        of libertinas and matronas to

your constructed demi-monde of pseudonyms

and pseudosex. Despite your impertinent

persistence, she's known more fucking passion from

a        .

### Friends, Romans, Countrymen
#### Rob Walton


never be afeard to use the


Fuck word when talking about him nor indeed
the fucking word nor yet the words  fuckable
and fuckery plus fucked would be fine or more
than fine but
remember
those other
words of importance to Catullus such as friends
and frivolity and faithfulness or plain faithful &
you might even want  to think about fighting or
fights and I
think   that
fresh-faced
clearly  has
its   merits
but the one
word above
all others is
what  we'll
call  the  F                              word

### Catullus in Libya
#### Andre Bagoo

At nights I removed my penis
but in the morning it grew whole again.
We sat at the shore, the sea's sulcus, & edged
into the light that burns the Sahara. Such women
that I love that I love such men: full of semen is my
purse, which pays the price and is paid in return.
I use them as if I had bought them for myself,
again and again their groins bursting
my anus
a flower at the furthest end of the desert
that ploughs through conquerors with petals.
Yet one day Libya I must flee, as I fled scorched
India, and deny the light that owns my soft marrow.
I will tell them of my love for her, this woman
of sand. My beheaded penis will not come
back like the sparrow on the cedar tree.
A bad rhyme I will be. Fuck me.

*(right) Catullus wordsearch*
*Tony Williams*

Learn more about
the ancient world with our

# CATULLUS
# WORDSEARCH

```
B R O N Z E B U T T O C K S S
O H L B S N O G G A T O S S L
L A T I N I T Y A F A C E M I
L A I T A P B X I T L K P O E
O V T H W S I F U M A R R Y P
C O S Y E Q L E S B I A G G I
K I S N E P Y L L I O N R I G
N D & I P D H C O M E S O M R
A A M A U F E H D O N G P P A
K N I C K E R S H L S P E R M
E A S T R O P H E O B O N E R
D L O V E F E A C L O D I A J
O R O M A N S E X T A P E S D
```

fun! late-classical! open-minded!

*Death & **Sex***
*Shauna Robertson*

## Before
he sees the
sack he's carrying,
tires of foreign service,
lies back after a large lunch,
bolts his rabbit-ridden outer door,
picks his own parsnips and feeds the vulture,

before he does
what's least and
easiest – rests a
creaking sandal on
the worn sill, hurls
work to the hobble-
footed God and
writes on the wind
and the running
water,

before he flings
off his tunic, stops
being thin, exhibits
his inner heirlooms,
frizzles on funereal
firewood and rocks
in his father's arms,

before his name is
touched with rust's
corrosion and he
touches nothing –

*(going up)*

*(going down)*

he'd like to dive
straight into her
foaming waves, scale
her Mount of Pipla,
get his namby-pamby
handies round her
iambics, graffiti the
frontage of her Randy
Inn,

he'd like to nose her
ninth pillar, stuff her
sitting tenants, bore
holes in her cloak,
bugger her gold-bearing
river,

he'd like to send his
fierce goat down her
Armpit Valley, fill up
his farmer's barns with
her fruits, drain dry
her fat soil of a swamp,
oh mother he'd like to

eat his way through her shoddy backstreets,
load up on her rural crudities, gobble
up her pungent cups, polish his
teeth with her piddle and
throw himself down
headlong from
her bending
bridge.

If someone
  let me go on kissing,
  I'd kiss three hundred
thousand times. A boy full
of wit and charm with salt
and wine.     A pretty girl in
her greenest flower – or any
tender kindling. Venuses &
Cupids. I'd kiss that creep
you've had your fill of and
that nice urbane man. New
bosses in scarlet thongs and
needy staff with baggage. The
Spanish. I'd kiss your sissy gobs
    and your not quite decent verses.
    Your long bridge and your rickety
    legs. That guest of yours. Clever
    dick lieutenants and your brother's
    hairy buttocks. A glutton, a gambler,
    nine uninterrupted thieves and (why
    not) Diana, unblemished – pure and
    unspoilt, with feet trussed up and
    backdoor open! Clodhoppers, boors.
    The Gods or something still more
    choice and fragrant – my comrade's
    small-scale monument! Fish, fowl, a
    black-throat crow, slave, spider, bug
    or fire – I'd kiss them all, good and
    long. All these poets, one large nose,
    the shoddy backstreet adulterers and,
    hell, anyone who cleans his teeth
    with water. You want to live
    on vulgar lips? You shall.
    I'll kiss the female fuck-up,
    friends and doctors, the
    pimp, the filthy trollop,
    any dove or nippy beak,
    bodies drier than horn.
    Windbags and contented
    brides. And yes, my darling,
    of course - your flabby
    little flanks, exactly
    to your liking.

Shauna Robertson

CCC

*Shauna Robertson*
*I*
*HATE & LOVE*

Perhaps you're asking why I do that?
I don't know, but I feel
it happening
and am

racked

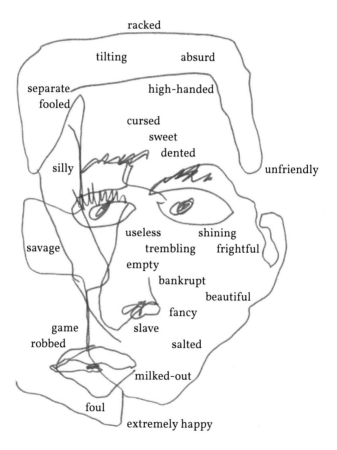

tilting          absurd

separate          high-handed
fooled

cursed
sweet
dented

silly                                    unfriendly

useless     shining
savage          trembling     frightful
empty
bankrupt
beautiful
fancy
game          slave
robbed          salted
milked-out
foul
extremely happy

your friend

## Shades of Canus & Schistaceus
### Shauna Robertson
*Using fragments from the translations by Guy Lee in* The Poems of Catullus
*(Oxford World's Classics, 2008)*

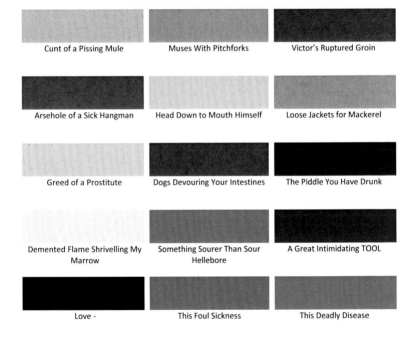

| | | |
|---|---|---|
| Cunt of a Pissing Mule | Muses With Pitchforks | Victor's Ruptured Groin |
| Arsehole of a Sick Hangman | Head Down to Mouth Himself | Loose Jackets for Mackerel |
| Greed of a Prostitute | Dogs Devouring Your Intestines | The Piddle You Have Drunk |
| Demented Flame Shrivelling My Marrow | Something Sourer Than Sour Hellebore | A Great Intimidating TOOL |
| Love - | This Foul Sickness | This Deadly Disease |

*Carmen*
*Peter Surkov*

That Valeria's a harvest worm

embellished with four limbs

and chatter from one end

I need not stress –

so are we all.

I merely say her mouth

and hindmost hole

compete in foulness.

Both issue filth

but welcome worse:

Marcus' questing tongue.

*Deep-set*
*Wanda O'Connor*
*(after Catullus 2, 14b & 26)*

sparrow
   [of the sea]
 making a sport of young things
  playing with one's whole cash box
she keeps, in curve        [cognate: a thing like a hawk]


   [with a whole mouth, public]
mimicry, the prime finger identifying,
enrobing sharp hurts     to hasten
       [the one more usually handsome]


                        – bizarre by accident, readers, you who
                          may trip upon and be rough with the

material by hands
  [uncomfortably between both    ]
           [as far as shaping may reach]
  [the sea jets
                   ] by means of wealth; a flourish
what lies, jest [jet]
what tiny luxury is in me    – her grief
  [vexed, vexing, ]
[
   lent beyond the surface   ]


                       – O infected and late gusts and gusting!
come rest, resting now my bloom, hot,
disconsolate [capella]
  [melancholic seamstress, marker of songs]
to smooth your agony I will play awhile…
   Acceptable to me is the upright [  ] girl with her golden apple
[thrown too high upon the mark]
   Acceptable to me: the woman's zone once fitted, freed.

## How Many Kisses?
### Kate Wise

Please show your working.

Running total:

| | | |
|---|---|---|
| one hundred | | 100 |
| one thousand | + | 1100 |
| a second hundred | + | 1200 |
| another thousand | + | 2200 |
| three hundred thousand | + | 302,200 |
| another | + | 302,201? |
| many | + | ? |
| many thousands | + | ?? |

= 

Many?

| | |
|---|---|
| | x |
| sweet as honey | x |
| without cease | x |
| losing count | x |

=

I'm lost

as many as
burning grains of Libyan sand
throbbing stars in the bruise-eyed night
as could be counted by jealous spies
as each swelling head of wheat in the August-ripe fields

=

Never enough.
Never, never enough.

### *CG Catullus*
*(The entire surviving oeuvre fed into a Markov chain text generator; the results then being translated into English. Selected extracts.)*

Oh best of the thieves and you, my house, my nose,
I may have slipped my silliness.

Perfume of the gods
slackened my fate.
My good intentions were sweet,
drawing out the weft when gazing on the girl.

We wished for the list, the loss of the bridge,
the breast of the voices.

Alas, he says the bottom, to himself that here, now here, now,
brings some to my old age.

For as far as she closes the chamber,
the woman will kiss weapons.

honey;
or words,
written by slow jerk, sure as sunset.

When you restore the page, Lesbia,
at the beginning of your eyes,
there is just so much.

# The Performers

An itinerant scribe, ROWYDA AMIN lived in the capital until she was sent into exile in the far west for an ill-judged remark about the emperor's hairpiece.
www.rowyda.com

Aside from his name, we know virtually nothing of poet ANDRE BAGOO. There is some suggestion his ancestors were from Libya and Asia. Centuries after his death, a vandal etched 'Bagoo' on Hadrian's Wall in Britannia beneath an image of Septimius Severus. @pleasureblog

VAHNI CAPILDEO may be found (but should not be looked for) in the thermæ, outdoor and indoor, at any hour and season, even in the extremes of Caledonia and Hibernia. Chiefly nocturnal and a devotee of Diana, she is currently working on an extended ekphrasis of the death of Actaeon, for ritual re-enactment.
@PerdutaGente

Having gambled away his meagre fortune at the circus maximus, JAMES COGHILL now makes a living as a soothsayer. He has pioneered a means of predicting what kind of syphilis one has, using only two rats, a fish rump and the little fingernail of an ostrogoth. A more virtuous doppelgänger of his blogs from time to time at:
thesolenette.wordpress.com

Born to the Brigantes, a Celtic tribe in Northern England, JEI DEGENHARDT traveled to Rome after Caesar's expedition to Britain in 55 BC. Jei met Catullus shortly before his death, who introduced them to his translations of Sappho. Unable to gain Roman citizenship, Jei spent the rest of their life retired in Lesbos, searching for lost papyrus fragments and writing poems about the 'man-womanish' god Bacchus.
@jeidegenhardt

The man known as CRAIG DOBSON is a scion of the faded Dobsonii family, whose ancestors drifted south of the that most August Emperor Hadrian's magnificent Wall during the troubled third century, Craigus found work as a teacher and comic actor but, being neither particularly learned nor amusing, he took a position with a family whose fortune had been made in business, and whose daughter found his combination of repetitive, tedious erudition and inappropriate *sphaerulaeque simul ioculatio* irresistible. Financially inept, and craving artistic recognition, he was last recorded selling graffito stencils for use (on the northern side only) of the Wall.

TIM DOOLEY, or Tmotheos, a slave with a Greek-sounding name, may in fact be the descendant of Hibernian pirates. He has troubled Londinium with obsequious critiques of our orators and a noxious book of verses Pēdita.

HARRY GILES is a Native of Ultima Thule, and as the ancient Aristophanes would have it, a Child of the Moon.
www.harrygiles.org

KIRSTEN IRVING managed to get through seven proclamations as Rome's herald until a gust of wind unmasked her as a woman. Thereafter she was banished to Britannia, where she went right back to her old ways, donning a horsehair moustache to join the labourers and making a pig's ear of a significant segment of Housesteads Fort.
@KoftheTriffids

ERIK KENNEDY is a citizen of Christopolis, Nova Zelandia. His work has recently appeared in papyri like *Landfall*, *The Literateur*, *Powder Keg Magazine*, *PUBLIC POOL*, and *The Rumpus*. He is the poetry editor for *Queen Mob's Teahouse* and a tribune of the plebs.
@thetearooms

As a married woman of noble birth KATHLEEN LATHAM organises the household and helps her husband with his correspondence. She enjoys the many pleasures that Rome has to offer. Her friends are impressed by her accurate readings of omens and her taking of the auspices. She is especially skilled in interpreting the flight of eagles and ravens. She worships the goddess Isis.

LINDSAY MACGREGOR, a member of the Caledonian Confederacy, is currently enjoying a one-month Proto-Pictish Ars Council residency in Rome, providing geopoetical advice to Julius Caesar on sources of gold beyond Gaul. She is an internationally-renowned tattoo artist, working mainly in woad.
@lindsaymacgreg1

IAN MCLACHLAN was the Republic's favourite tragedian. Due to an unfortunate incident involving Pompey's son-in-law and the Cloaca Maxima, Ian now lives in remote Britain where he is a student of Stoicism and an assiduous writer of curse tablets.
@ianjmclachlan

A nomad of extremely mixed origin, GABRIELLE NOLAN was raised on the island of Themiscyra and later instructed in the ways of Satavahan sages. She appreciates the anonymity and extravagance of a poet's life in the capital.
@gabsadora

WANDA O'CONNOR: "In this age of fictions it is pleasing to us, the housed-in poetae, to reach the mouths of vulgaris. In a manner suitable to our work, the words making a sudden attack do snatch the entrails. Offering up the half-raw and endeavouring to suck out the poisons of ill fit, I write."
@misswandalynn

ABI PALMER is a model citizen. She likes to trample wine underfoot, pluck out the choicest grapes and pop them straight into her mouth using her purpled toes. All this while throned on the communal shitter.
www.abipalmer.com

ABIGAIL PARRY attends revels and drinking parties by night in the Forum, and even upon the Rostra. Pliny the Elder has described her as an *exemplum licentiae*. @ginpitnancy

EILEEN PUN was a sword-carrying and lute-playing wanderer who slipped between Roman towns, cities, and countryside until she was asked to pay the Aes Uxorium tax (on unmarried men or woman who could bear children), or face exile. Unable to comply, she was made to give up her sword, but allowed to keep her instrument and was sent to the unprotected, cold and rainy settlement near Fort Galava in the far north west of Britannia. During a raid, she proved her skill with weapons and was given an honorary place in the infantry as keeper of the armoury.

SHAUNA ROBERTSON was born in the shadow of Hadrian's Wall in the year 1968 AD, forcing a blush from the brazen adulteress with a face like a Gallican goat's. With long fingers and a dry mouth, her future as a carp-seizer seemed assured until a plague of backstreet rabbits

tragically cut short her tone, tactics and aspirations of depravity.
http://shaunarobertson.wordpress.com

JON STONE is an augur, originally from Derventio Coritanorum, with a singular reputation for inaccuracy – likely due to the fact that he frequently loses control of his cat, Bustus, when taking the auspices. www.gojonstonego.com

PETER SURKOV, a student of Asclepiades, maintains his absence from the capital, but sends fond greetings to his friends and creditors. @_surkov

ANDREA TALLARITA (Floruit AD 110-150) is believed to have been born in Parthenope (modern Naples). A boy actor and aulos player for itinerant Roman drama, by uncertain circumstances he went on to train as a jurist under Gaius. Recent studies (Hagestedt) suggest he may have served up to three Praetorian prefects of Gaul throughout his lifetime. His writings were considered for, but ultimately not included in, Theodosius II's Lex citationum.
www.marjacq.com/andrea-tallarita.html

CLAIRE TRÉVIEN was elected dictator for life in 60 BC, and intends to use the role to beat the world record for most grapes eaten in 24hours. http://clairetrevien.co.uk

INGA VESPERIA always has her stylus at the ready, even when she's soaking in Bath or traipsing the Britannian hills from Verulamium to Birdoswalda. Of Langobardian origin, she lives in Londinium, near the hill where dreaded Boudicca hid her troops of smelly Brittunculi; it now makes an excellent spot from which to enjoy the view and eat a spiced partridge.
@keeping_cool

ROB WALTON was recently unjustly sacked from his position as Professor of Rhetoric, and now runs spoken word nights at the Atrium Poetica (Martha's Bar, weekly), Collis Palatium (Millie's Bar, monthly) and Lazio FC (Supporters' Bar, once in a luna caerulea). He wears his toga to the right and spends too much time in the tepidarium.
@anicelad

TONY WILLIAMS is the anglicised name of Antoninus Cornelius Gaius Terrahorn Willahelm Quintus, a Stoic and mud-seller associated with the circle of Cinna. Although a Roman citizen, the Germanic Willahelm ('helmet of desire') indicates at least a partially barbaric lineage. He seems to have been vengefully penetrated by Catullus, either in person or with a stick of white asparagus, after an argument over whether Lesbia's breasts looked more like goose eggs or pomegranates. He appears in Shakespeare's lost play *Done Romans* as Antonionio, a pathetic drunk who can't make up his mind who to stab. @TonyWilliams9

KATE WISE divides her time between the roles of materfamilias and advocatrix. Rescued from the provinces, she has been educated, and has ideas, above her station. She still prefers Sappho's *31* to Catullus' *51*.

JENNIFER WONG is a weaver from Han Dynasty China. She chose her profession over trading and sorcery, both of which are considered highly immoral.
jenniferwong.co.uk

# *Acknowledgements*

In addition to the texts cited throughout this compendium, we would like to acknowledge:

- Roger Pearse's online collection of translations of classical texts at www.tertullian.org
- The paintings on the walls of the surburban baths and brothels of Pompeii for inspiring our *Carmina Sutra*
- easyJet's in-flight duty-free catalogue
- Ben Davis from the Noun Project for the battleaxes.
- Lele Saa from the Noun Project for the umbrella
- Sophia Lee from the Noun Project for the dagger
- lostandtaken.com for various textures
- Obsidian Dawn for the bullet holes
- Hay Kranen for the PHP Markov generator
- Ian McLachland and Craig Dobson for the graffiti

# *Further Reading*

- 'Passer Mortuus Est' by Edna St. Vincent Millay

- *Carmen LXIV* by Simon Smith (Knives, Forks and Spoons, 2012)

- *Catulla et al* by Tiffany Atkinson (Bloodaxe, 2011)

- *Catullus: Poems of Love and Hate* by Josephine Balmer (Bloodaxe, 2004)

- *Catullus: Fragmenta* by Louis Zukofsky and Celia Zukovsky (Jonathan Cape, 1969) – homophonic versions.

**Add your own recommendations below**
*(After all, you might hand this book on some day.)*